THE LIFE CYCLE OF THE
ROYAL ALBATROSS

Betty Brownlie

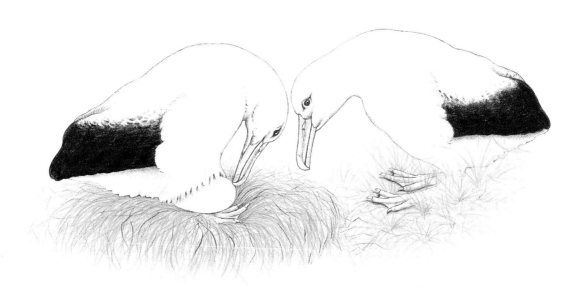

SCHOLASTIC
Auckland Sydney New York London Toronto
Mexico City New Delhi Hong Kong

Acknowledgements

The author wishes to thank most sincerely Television New Zealand's *Wild South* Natural History Unit, and Beverly Brown, producer of the royal albatross documentary film *Grandma*, for use of film footage for research.

The publisher gratefully acknowledges the assistance of the Literature Programme of the QEII Arts Council in the publication of this book.

First published by Ashton Scholastic, 1995
Reprinted by Scholastic New Zealand Limited
Private Bag 94407, Greenmount, Auckland 1730, New Zealand

Scholastic Australia Pty Limited
PO Box 579, Gosford, NSW 2250, Australia

Scholastic Inc
555 Broadway, New York, NY 10012-3999, USA

Scholastic Limited
1-19 New Oxford Street, London, WC1A 1NU, England

Scholastic Canada Limited
175 Hillmount Rd, Markham, Ontario L6C 1Z7, Canada

Scholastic Mexico
Bretana 99, Col. Zacahuitzco, 03550, Mexico D.F., Mexico

Scholastic India Pte Limited
29 Udyog Vihar, Phase-1, Gurgaon-122 016, Haryana, India

Scholastic Hong Kong Limited
Room 601-2, Tung Shun Hing Commercial Centre,
20-22 Granville Road, Kowloon, Hong Kong

© Betty Brownlie, 1995

Cataloguing-in-Publication Data

Brownlie, Betty.
The life cycle of the royal albatross / by Betty Brownlie.
Auckland, N.Z.: Ashton Scholastic, 1994.
1 v. (Read by reading)
ISBN: 1-86943-202-9
1. Readers--Birds. I. Title. II. Title: Royal Albatross III. Series:
Read by reading series
428.6

11 10 9 8 7 6 5 4 3   2 3 4 5 6 7 / 0

Edited by Penny Scown
Typeset in 14/16 Garamond by Designer Graphix
Printed in Hong Kong

Contents

INTRODUCTION

The royal albatross is the largest seabird in the world. It measures up to 1.35 metres from bill to tail, and has a giant wing span of 3 metres or more. It may weigh 7.5 kilograms, and can carry 15% of its weight in food. The royal albatross is also among the longest-living birds, commonly living for 30–40 years. One is even known to have been still producing young into her 60s!

Famous for long-distance gliding, the royal albatross spends more than 80 percent of its life at sea. It only returns to land once every two years to breed. Taiaroa Head, on the east coast of New Zealand's South Island, is the only mainland albatross colony in the world. Other breeding colonies are on offshore islands in the southern Pacific Ocean.

There are two groups of royal albatrosses; the southern royal albatross is slightly larger than the northern one, and it breeds mainly on the more southern sub-antarctic island groups, namely the Auckland Islands and Campbell Island.

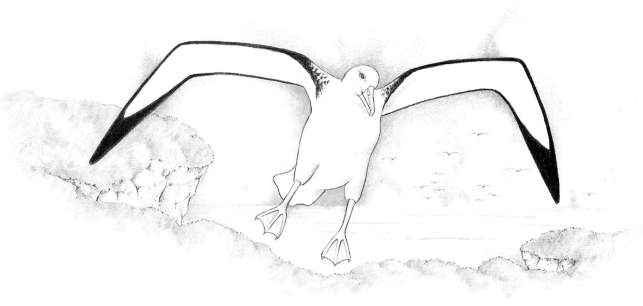

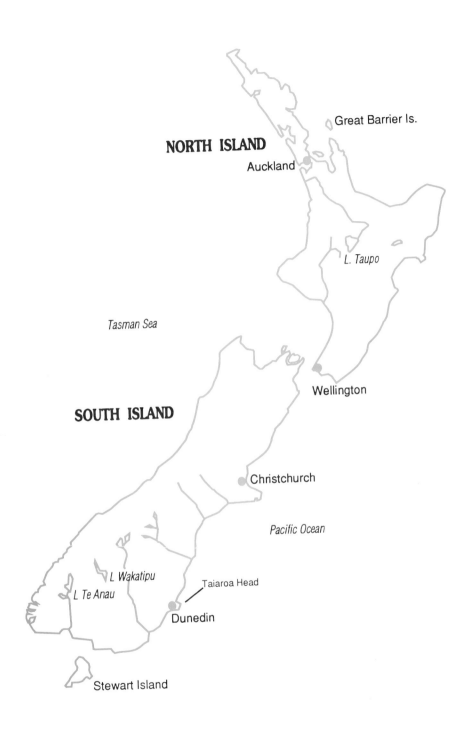

NORTH ISLAND

Great Barrier Is.

Auckland

L. Taupo

Tasman Sea

SOUTH ISLAND

Wellington

Christchurch

Pacific Ocean

L Wakatipu

Taiaroa Head

L Te Anau

Dunedin

Stewart Island

Auckland Islands

Campbell Island

5

What ROYAL ALBATROSSES LOOK LIKE

Feathers

The royal albatross has mainly white **plumage** (feathers) with black feathers on the upper surface of its wings.

At the base of its tail is an oil gland. The albatross uses its bill and the back of its head to squeeze oil droplets from this gland, which it then spreads throughout its feathers. This is thought to have a conditioning, waterproofing effect.

Although it is a water bird, the albatross must still bathe to clean its feathers and keep them in good condition.

Old, worn feathers fall out from time to time throughout the year and new feathers quickly grow to replace them. This is called **moulting** and it happens gradually, so that the albatross can still keep warm. Slow moulting also means that the bird's ability to glide is not affected.

Albatross preening

Albatross bathing

Bill and Mouth

The albatross has a strong, hooked upper bill for grasping its food. The trough-like lower bill is necessary for chicks to catch the liquified food the adults bring them. Both bills have sharp edges for cutting large food such as squid into smaller pieces.

   The lower bill is hinged so that the bird can open its mouth extremely wide. The albatross's tongue and parts of its mouth are rough to help the bird grasp and eat slippery seafood.

   Inside the albatross's head are two large salt glands. Excess salt from the bird's seafood diet is got rid of through tube-like nostrils near the base of the top bill. The salty liquid runs down a groove on each side of the bill, forming a drip on the end. The albatross may shake its head now and then to shake off the drip.

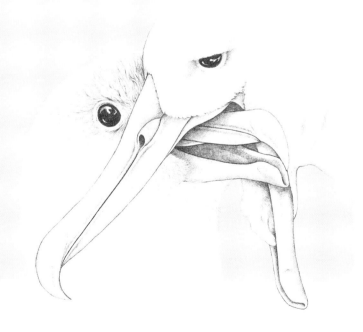

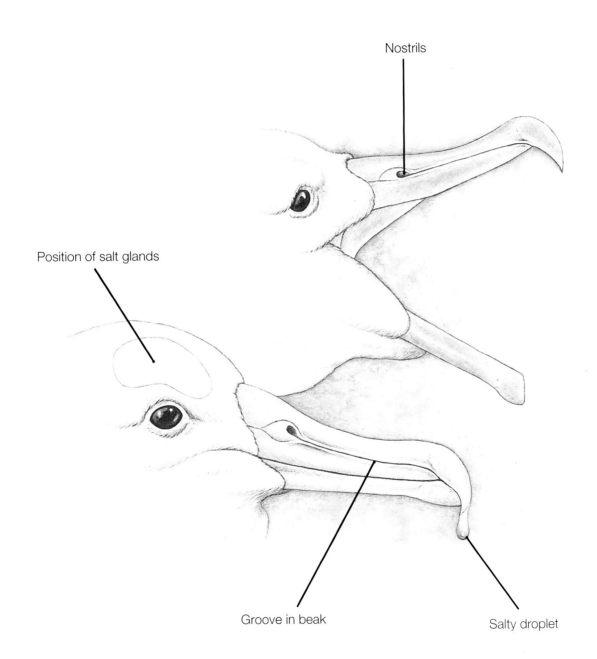

Nostrils

Position of salt glands

Groove in beak

Salty droplet

Ears

A bird's sense of hearing is very well developed. Each ear is a hole on the side of the bird's head, behind the eyes. The holes are covered by feathers, which cut out the sound of the wind whistling by as the bird flies but do not muffle sounds the bird needs to hear.

Eyes

Birds have an upper and lower eyelid, as well as a clear, protective eyelid called the **nictating membrane**. This membrane may be drawn across the eyes like a window. Albatrosses flying for days at a time may cover their eyes with the nictating membrane, especially in stormy weather.

Legs and Feet

The albatross has strong, lightweight leg bones and large, webbed feet. On land, the albatross waddles clumsily on its big feet, but in water the webbed toes help the bird swim very fast.

Wings and Flight

As with all flying birds, the albatross's bones are thin and lightweight. Most are hollow and crisscrossed with fine struts for strength, rather like a honeycomb. This means that the bird's skeleton is not too heavy for flight.

Birds also have extensions to their lungs, called **air sacs**. These are linked to many of the air spaces within the bones of the skeleton, so when the bird breathes, air travels throughout its body. This amazing breathing system enables the albatross to sustain long-distance flight, and fly in high altitudes where the air is thin.

The albatross glides, rarely using a wing beat, on journeys of thousands of kilometres around the remote southern oceans. Using a special tendon, the bird is able to lock its wings into a rigid (stiff) position. It can then glide effortlessly, without getting tired, at speeds of up to 115 kilometres per hour for very long periods with barely a flap of its wings. The albatross's swoop speed is at least 140 kilometres per hour.

Since albatrosses spend 80 percent of their time at sea, flying or gliding is a very important part of their lives.

Gliding into the wind allows the albatross to retain height. But the headwind also causes it to lose forward speed. Before it stalls and falls from the sky, however, the albatross swoops downwards, towards the ocean. Then it soars skywards, which increases its glide speed again. The action is rather like a roller coaster rushing downhill, then shooting up the other side. (See 'Gliding' opposite.)

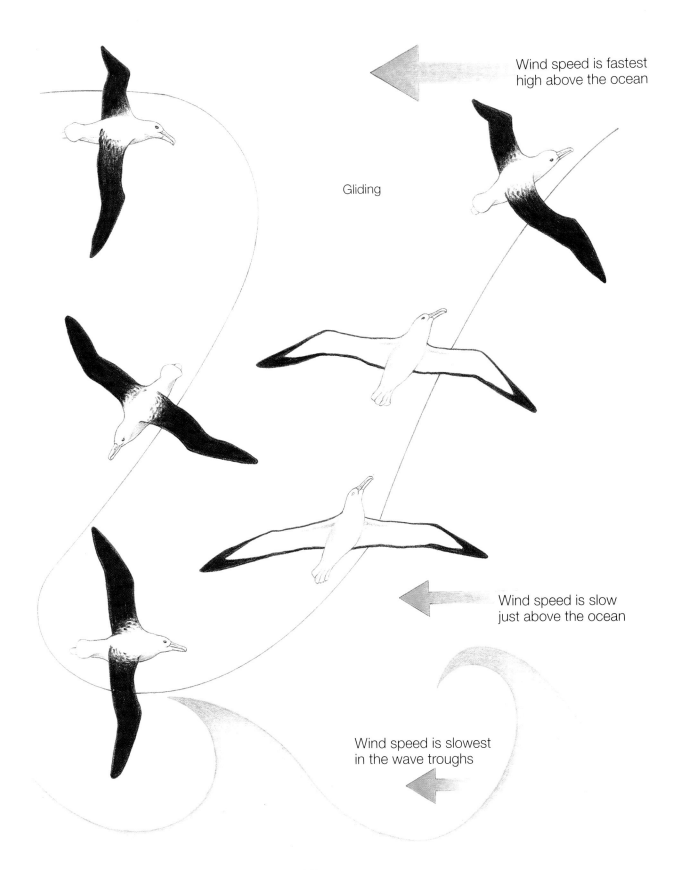

Gliding

Wind speed is fastest
high above the ocean

Wind speed is slow
just above the ocean

Wind speed is slowest
in the wave troughs

Taking off

The albatross's runway for take-off usually slopes downhill from the nest site to a windswept cliff edge, high above the sea. If there is no wind at the usual take-off site, the bird may walk for many hours searching for another suitably windy cliff. To take off, the albatross simply walks or runs off the edge of the cliff. The wind catches beneath its outstretched wings and it glides out to sea.

To take off from the water, the albatross faces into the wind, flaps its wings and paddles furiously with its huge webbed feet, running on top of the water.

Taking off from water

Taking off from land

Landing

To land, the albatross faces into the wind, tilting its body downwards to catch the wind and help reduce speed. It uses its legs and tail to steer and balance itself, and spreads its huge webbed feet to act like brakes against the wind. As it loses speed it must flap its wings to stop it from falling from the sky like a stone.

If there is no wind, the bird won't be able to brake effectively and may crash-land. If the wind is too strong or gusty on the other hand, the buffeting may cause birds to collide in mid-air, or to land awkwardly. A broken wing is the albatross's death sentence.

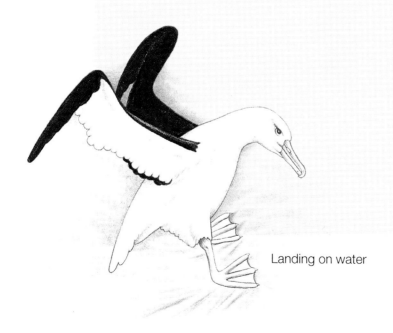

Landing on water

Crash-landing

Life cycle
of the
Royal Albatross

During the month of October, albatrosses begin to return to the breeding colonies from far out at sea. Often, the male arrives first and awaits the return of his mate. The female arrives anything from a few hours to several weeks later.

Previously unmated birds, or those who have lost their mates, gather together in noisy, excited gatherings called **gams**. They 'display' to each other and practise courtship rituals in the hope of one day attracting a mate. Although they rarely breed before the age of 9 or 10 years, they are on the lookout for a suitable partner several years before that.

Nest-building

The male albatross may have built a nest before his mate arrives at the colony. If she does not approve of his efforts, she may build another nest herself.

The nest is built on level ground, as close as is practical to the cliff edge from which the birds fly out to sea to feed. The completed nest, made of grasses and surrounding debris, looks like a low mound with the centre hollowed out.

Courtship

As albatrosses usually mate for life, they will generally display the entire courtship dance only once in their lives, between two birds who will then become bonded. The dance is accompanied by much shrieking, whistling, wheezing, honking, and clacking of bills. The display may last for up to half an hour.

Mating

When the female albatross arrives at the colony, she already has her single egg developing inside her. She must mate with her partner while her egg is at a certain stage of development, otherwise no chick will grow inside the egg. The two birds therefore mate frequently over several days to ensure the egg is fertilised.

When mating is completed, both birds fly out to sea to feed. The female will sometimes stay at sea for about 10 days, until she is almost ready to lay her egg.

All the albatrosses will have laid their eggs by mid to late November.

Preparing to mate

Female

Male

Female

Male

The courtship dance
Usually the male albatross dances first,
offering himself to the female.
Then the female joins in
and dances her acceptance.

21

Incubation

Breeding albatrosses — male and female — develop a special **brood patch** on their bellies. This is a patch where the feathers have fallen out. Beneath the patch of bare skin there is now a concentration of blood vessels. This ensures that the brood patch is very warm, as this is the part that will lie over the egg during **incubation** (the period when the birds sit on the egg before it hatches).

Average incubation time is 79 days, during which the parent birds take turns at sitting on the egg.

Hatching

Usually, albatross eggs hatch in late January/early February. About 70 days from when the egg was laid, the chick can be heard calling faintly from inside. From the time it first breaks the shell, it may take 3–4 days for the chick to hatch out completely. The adults do not help it, and if it takes too long, the chick will die.

The newly hatched chick's wet, spiky feathers will dry in about 12 hours. The resulting soft, fluffy white chick has pink skin showing through its down, and its bill and feet are pinkish-grey.

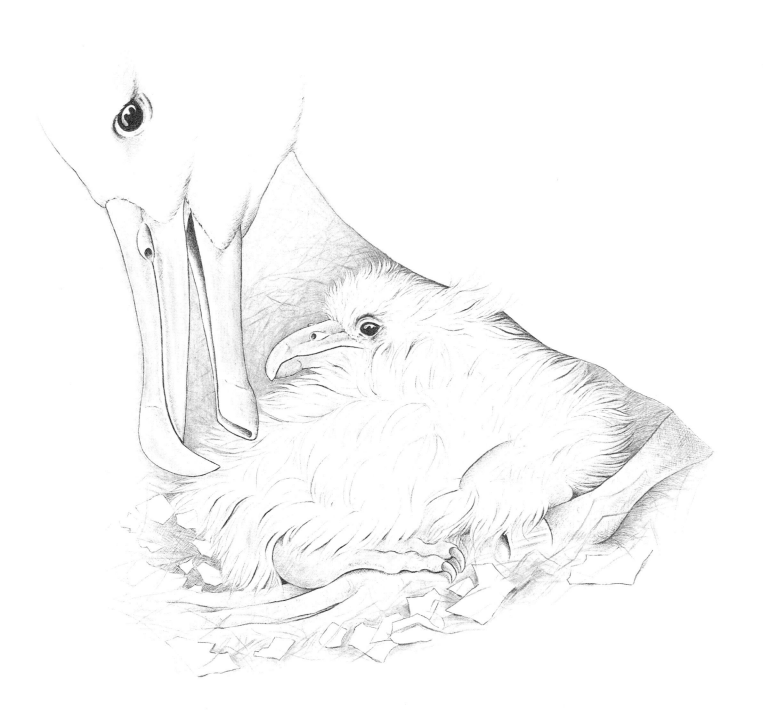

Brooding

The brooding period lasts five weeks. The adults take turns at sitting over the small bird, keeping it safe and warm beneath their brood patches.

For the first three weeks, the chick is fed daily. For the following two weeks it is fed every second day. The adults feed the chick by **regurgitating** (coughing up) food that they have swallowed and stored in their **crop**, a large storage sac where food becomes softened. They also regurgitate a special nutritious oil which may be mixed with the stored food, making a mushy seafood soup.

By early autumn (March), the adults will leave the chick on the nest, unguarded, for short periods while they both fly out to sea to feed themselves and to gather food for the chick.

By late autumn/early winter (May/June), the chick is ready to be left entirely unguarded, except for brief visits once a week by a parent bringing food. The chick has grown dramatically. It is now kept warm by a thick layer of body fat beneath the down, and later by its developing feathers. By midwinter (July), hard black wing feathers are growing amidst the remaining down.

Finally, by late winter/early spring (August/September), at about 7 months of age, the young bird is the size of its giant parents. It will be fed day and night by both parents to speed up its final stages of development.

For the first 5 weeks of its life
the chick is constantly brooded
by one of its parents

By 7 months of age, the young bird
has reached the size of its parents

Fledging (first flight)

By spring (September), the adult birds will have gradually reduced their offspring's food supply, causing it to lose weight. The fledgling albatross now looks like its parents. It begins to spend most of its time stretching and flapping its wings, building up its flight muscles and improving its coordination.

As the time nears for the young albatross to fly from the colony, the adults will stop feeding it altogether. It will not eat again until it catches its own food out at sea.

Finally, 8–9 months after hatching, the chick is ready to fly. To ensure its body carries no unnecessary weight for its first flight, the young bird regurgitates the remaining contents of its stomach.

There are no practice take-offs and no trial flights. Nor do the adults give any flying lessons. The young albatross simply leans into the wind and launches itself off the clifftop. Its great wings flap briefly then lock into their rigid glide position. The young albatross heads out to sea. It will not walk on land again for 3–5 years.

Most of the fledglings will have left the colony by the end of September, with the last few leaving in early October, just as the next season's males begin to arrive to breed.

WHAT ROYAL ALBATROSSES EAT

The royal albatross's diet consists solely of seafood, mainly squid. It also eats fish, and will readily take octopus and fish scraps that are dumped at sea by fishing boats.

   The albatross flies too fast to scoop food from the water while flying, as many birds do. Instead, it must land on the water and swim towards to the food it has seen from the air. It ducks its head into the water to catch its prey.

THREATS TO THE ROYAL ALBATROSS

On the mainland colony, land predators such as rats and ferrets are a threat to eggs and chicks.

Mid-air collisions between albatrosses can occur above crowded breeding colonies. Although the crashes are not often fatal, if a bird breaks a wing it is doomed to die as it will not be able to fly or feed itself.

Unexpected shifts in ocean currents may disrupt the albatrosses' usual feeding grounds. Young, inexperienced birds may then find it difficult to find food, and starve.

However, possibly the albatrosses' worst enemy is humankind. Toxic chemical waste and oil spills endanger both the albatrosses and their feeding grounds at sea.

Rubbish and plastic floating on the ocean may be picked up by the birds, and even fed to the chicks.

Many albatrosses die when they try to snatch bait from fishing lines being towed behind trawlers and they become hooked or tangled in the lines.

Albatrosses usually breed on desolate islands, often losing from 25-75 percent of eggs and new chicks. However, at Taiaroa Head, on the New Zealand coast, wardens help ensure the albatrosses' breeding success. So although some people may be responsible for the loss of many adult albatrosses, it is encouraging to know that others are helping save the chicks.

INDEX

BIBLIOGRAPHY

AA Book of New Zealand Wildlife. Auckland, Lansdowne Press 1981.
Bryant, Donna; illustrated by Julie Roil. *The Wildtrack Book*.
   Auckland, Hodder & Stoughton 1990.
Complete Book of New Zealand Birds. Reader's Digest 1985.
Dalton, Stephen. *The Miracle of Flight*. Maidenhead, Sampson Low 1977.
Gaskin, Chris & Neville Peat; photographs by Kim Westerkov.
   The World of Albatrosses. Auckland, Hodder & Stoughton 1991.
Jacobs, Warren. *New Zealand Birds*. Christchurch, Kowhai Publishing 1983.
Sage, Bryan; photographs by Eric Hosking. *Antarctic Wildlife*. Whitcoulls 1982.
Turbott, E.G. *Bullers Birds of New Zealand*. Christchurch, Whitcoulls 1967.